GROWING ROSES

The beginner's guide to growing Rose plants from varieties to harvesting

Davies Cheruiyot

GROWING ROSES

Copyright © 2024 Davies Cheruiyot

All rights reserved.

CONTENTS

Acknowledgments

1 INTRODUCTION TO GROWING ROSES

Introduction

Benefits

2 ROSE PLANT VARIETIES

Hybrid Tea Roses

Floribunda Roses

Grandiflora Roses

Polyantha Roses

Shrub Roses

Climbing Roses

Miniature Roses

English Roses

3 ROSE PLANTS GROWING REQUIREMENTS

Light and Temperature

Soil

Propagation

Fertilizer

Water

Cultural Practices

Harvesting

4 ROSE PLANTS PESTS AND DISEASES

Scales

Spider Mites

White Flies

Mealybugs

Thrips

Powdery Mildew

Downey Mildew

Fusarium Wilt

Crown Gall

Nematodes

ACKNOWLEDGMENTS

I would like to express my gratitude to all people who helped me in editing and finalizing the final draft of this book

1 INTRODUCTION TO GROWING ROSES

Introduction

Rose is a perennial flowering plant from the family of Rosaceae and are native to North America, Asia and Europe. There are several species of rose plants with most of them being grown as cut flowers and for ornamental purposes.

Roses are majorly grown as cut flowers in making bouquets or gift presentation but they can as well be planted for ornamental purposes.

Rose plants produce pinnately and alternate leaves with 2 to 5 flower petals depending on the cultivar planted. Rose plants produces berries which range from orange to red in color.

Benefits

Rose petals can be distilled with steam to produce rose water which can have the following benefits;

Soothing skin irritation

Rose water contain anti-inflammatory components which may help in soothing skin irritation.

Cell protection

Rose water contain high antioxidants which may help in cell protection.

Healing burns and wounds

Rose water contain anti-inflammatory properties which may help in healing burns and wounds.

Reduces stress

Rose water contains antianxiety compounds which may help in reducing stress levels in the body.

2 ROSE PLANT VARIETIES

VARIETIES

There are several varieties of roses but you should ensure that you select the right rose variety that is popular in several parts of the world. There are several varieties of roses and categorizing them will be good for identifying them easily. Roses can be categorized based on blooms, color and so forth. The following are the most common categories of roses;

1. Hybrid Tea Roses
2. Floribunda Roses
3. Grandiflora Roses
4. Polyantha Roses
5. Shrub Roses
6. Climbing Roses
7. Miniature Roses
8. English Roses

1. Hybrid Tea Roses

GROWING ROSES

Hybrid Tea roses are the most common rose types amongst other roses. Hybrid Tea Roses produce long stems and blooms which are resistant to pests and diseases.

GROWING ROSES

The most common Hybrid Tea roses are;

- Tahitian Sunset Rose
- Elle Rose

2. Floribunda Roses

GROWING ROSES

Floribunda roses are rose plants which produce huge blooms in clusters and can easily be grown and are easy to maintain.

GROWING ROSES

The most common floribunda roses are;

- Cherry Parfait Rose
- Easy Does It Rose
- Mardi Gras Rose
- Morden Fireglow Rose
- Julia Child Rose

3. Grandiflora Roses

Grandiflora roses are a subgroup of hybrid tea roses that produce tall rose plants and flowers that appear in clusters. The most common grandiflora roses are;

- About Face Rose
- Wild Blue Yonder Rose

4. Polyantha Roses

Polyantha roses are rose plants with short stems and blooms and are mostly used for ornamental purposes.

5.　Shrub Roses

Shrub roses are rose plants with sprawling growing rates and can grow to a height of 10 feet when they have fully matured. The most common shrub roses are;

- Bonica Roses
- Teasing Georgia Rose
- Falstaff Roses
- Rainbow Knockout Roses

6. Climbing Roses

Climbing roses also referred to as rambling roses are rose plants with long canes are mostly used along trellis and fences.

7. Miniature Roses

Miniature roses are rose plants with compact growth rates and compact blooms and can grow to a height of 14 feet tall.

8. English Roses

English roses are hardy rose plants with a wide range of bloom colors and beautiful scents.

The most common rose plant varieties are;

1. About Face Roses
2. Cherry Parfait Roses
3. Falstaff Roses
4. Mardi Gras Roses
5. Wild Blue Yonder Roses
6. Elle Roses
7. Morden Fireglow Roses
8. Frankly Scarlet Roses
9. Tahitian Sunset Roses
10. Rainbow Knockout Roses
11. Julia Child Roses
12. Teasing Georgia Roses
13. Easy Does It Roses
14. Bonica Roses

1. About Face Roses

GROWING ROSES

About Face are rose plants from grandiflora rose category that produces greenish leaves, long stems and orange blooms.

About Face rose plants are resistant to pests and diseases and can grow to a height of 6 fee when fully established.

You should plant About Face rose plants under full sunlight and well drained soils which are high in organic matter.

2. Cherry Parfait Roses

GROWING ROSES

Cherry Parfait Roses are rose plants from floribunda rose category with dark greenish foliage and white blooms.

Cherry Parfait rose plants should be planted between zones 5 to 11 under full sunlight and well drained soil types.

Cherry Parfait rose plants have bushy growth rates and can grow to a height of 4 feet when mature.

3. Falstaff Roses

Falstaff Roses are rose plants from shrub rose categories that produce red crimson blooms.

Falstaff rose plants should be planted between zones 5 to 11 under full sunlight and well drained soils which are high in organic matter.

4. Mardi Gras Roses

GROWING ROSES

Mardi Gras Roses are rose plans from floribunda rose category with multicolor blooms that range from yellow, pink and orange. Mardi Grass rose plants produce dark greenish blooms and sweet blooms when they are planted under full sunlight.

You should plant Mardi Gras rose plants between zones 5 to 9 and under well drained and moist soils.

5. Wild Blue Yonder Roses

GROWING ROSES

Wild Blue Yonder Roses are rose plants from grandiflora rose categories which produces lavender blooms in large clusters.

You should plant Wild Blue Yonder roses between zones 5 to 9 under full sunlight and loamy soils that are well drained and moist.

6. Elle Roses

GROWING ROSES

Elle Roses are rose plants from Hybrid Tea rose categories which produces citrus like aromas.

You should plant Elle roses between zones 5 to 9 under full sunlight and sandy soils which are well drained and moist.

7. Morden Fireglow Roses

GROWING ROSES

Morden Fireglow Roses are rose plants from floribunda rose categories that produce matte foliage and red and orange blooms.

Morden Fireglow roses are mostly used as cut flowers and should be planted between zones 3 to 9 under full sunlight and well drained soils which are rich in organic matter.

8. Frankly Scarlet Roses

Frankly Scarlet Roses are rose plants from floribunda rose category that produces dark greenish foliage and sweet bloom aroma.

You should plant Frankly Scarlet rose plants under full sunlight and well drained soils preferably between zones 5 to 9.

9. Tahitian Sunset Roses

GROWING ROSES

Tahitian Sunset Roses are rose plants with bi-color blooms that tend to have anise smell. These rose plants produce dark greenish leaves and beautiful blooms which are resistant to diseases.

You should plant Tahitian Sunset rose plants between zones 6 to 11 under well drained soils and full sunlight.

10. Rainbow Knockout Roses

Rainbow Knockout Roses are rose plants from shrub rose category which produce dark greenish leaves and blooms in clusters.

You should plant Rainbow Knockout roses between zones 4 to 9 under fertile soils that are well drained. Rainbow Knockout roses can grow to a height of 4 feet when they are planted under full sunlight.

11. Julia Child Roses

GROWING ROSES

Julia Child Roses are rose plants from floribunda categories with glossy foliage and sweet smelling blooms which appear in clusters.

Julia Child rose plants thrive well between zones 5 to 11 under most soil types as long as they are well drained and moist. Julia Child rose plants should be planted under full sunlight with the plant growing to a height of 5 feet when they are fully established.

12. Teasing Georgia Roses

Teasing Georgia Roses are rose plants from shrub rose category with small blooms in clusters. You should plant Teasing Georgia rose plants between zones 5 to 11 under full sunlight and well drained soils which are high in organic matter.

13. Easy Does It Roses

Easy Does It Roses are rose plants from floribunda rose categories which produce bushy growth rates and pink orange blooms that have sweet aroma.

You should plant Easy Does It rose plants between zones 5 to 11 under full sunlight and well draining soils.

14. Bonica Roses

Bonica Roses are rose plants from shrub rose category that produces sprawling growth rates and light pinkish blooms when mature.

GROWING ROSES

GROWING ROSES

Bonica rose plants thrive well in cool climatic conditions and can be planted between zones 3 to 11. Bonica rose plants should be planted under full sunlight and well drained soils which are rich in organic matter.

3 ROSE PLANTS GROWING REQUIREMENTS

GROWING REQUIREMENTS OF ROSES

Light and temperature

Rose plants perform well under full sunlight and therefore you should make sure that they receive an average of 6 to 8 hours of light per day.

Rose plants perform well moderate and humid climatic conditions that range from 15 degrees Celsius to 28 degrees Celsius.

Soil

Rose plants perform well in soils that are rich in organic matter and are well drained. Rose plants require soils that have a P.H range of 6.0 to 6.5.

Propagation

Rose plants are propagated by cuttings method. You will require sharp scissors to cut the stem cuttings. Follow these simple steps to propagate them successfully;

- Cut stems below the node that has an average length of 5 inches.
- Remove the lower part of the leaves and place them in a rooting hormone.
- Prepare potting mix and plant the cuttings.
- Place the cuttings in a warm, dry place that can receive an average of 6 to 8 hours of sunlight.
- Transplant the new plants into large containers or permanent garden after three weeks.

Fertilizers

Roses are heavy feeders and they should therefore be provided with balanced fertilizers of nitrogen, phosphorus and potassium so that they can produce more quality blooms. Applying foliar and soluble fertilizers to rose plants will help them in their overall growth.

Water

Rose plants like several plants require water for them to attain optimal growth rates. Newly planted rose plants should be provided with an average of 1 to 2 inches of water on weekly basis so that their roots can get established easily. Fully established rose plants do not require water so much. They should be watered once In a while when the soils are dry and during prolonged drought season.

Cultural practices

Bending

Rose plants require bending so that the plants can attain healthy growth rates and to keep them from pests and diseases. Bending should be done 6 to 8 weeks after you have transplanted your rose plants and this should be done continually during their growing season. You should do bending 3 to 5 cm from the ground so that new and healthy stems can be able to grow.

Mulching

Mulching is an important cultural practice to rose plants. Mulching will help rose plants in conservation of moisture content in the soil, prevention of soil erosion and suppression of weeds.

Disbudding

Disbudding is the process of removing side buds of roses to encourage apical dominance. Disbudding should be done consistently so that rose plants can be able to produce quality blooms.

Defoliation

Defoliation is an important cultural practice which helps in improving aeration within the plants thus reducing possible spread of diseases. You should therefore remove old, dry and leaves that have been infected to give room for new growths.

Gapping

Gapping is the process of replacing rose plants that have failed to establish so that the intended production rates are achieved.

De-suckering

De-suckering entails the process of removing buds that have overgrown on a single stem to reduce competition for the same nutrients and to help in production of more blooms.

Weeding

Rose plants require proper weeding so that the plants can grow with the right nutrients. Weeds if not removed can compete with rose plants for nutrients and light resulting in the plants not attaining the required quality standards.

Harvesting

GROWING ROSES

Rose plants that are newly planted can be harvested 55 days after planting them. You should harvest stems that have between 44 to 58cm above by cutting them at 1cm in height and this should be done above 2 leaf nodes.

Rose stems should be harvested by use of sharp pruners when rose plants have fully attained their color. You should harvest roses early in the morning or late in the evening so as to preserve the moisture in the stems.

Harvesting tools should be disinfected before cutting rose stems and after cutting them by use of chlorine solution. This is an important practice to perform to prevent diseases like Crown Gall which can easily destroy your cut roses.

Post-harvesting

Rose stems that have been harvested should be placed in post-harvesting solution before they are cooled.

Bunching

Rose stems should be bunched according to their size and you can place them in a bunch of 9 to 11 stems.

Sleeving

Rose stems meant for transportation should be sleeved by use of fennel shaped polythene sleeves.

Packing and transportation

Roses should be packed in carton boxes and placed in vehicles that have cold facilities since rose stems can easily wither if not maintained under right conditions.

4 ROSE PLANTS PESTS AND DISEASES

ROSE PLANTS PESTS AND DISEASES

The most common pests and diseases that may affect rose plants are;

1. Scales
2. Spider Mites
3. White Flies
4. Mealybugs
5. Thrips
6. Powdery Mildew
7. Downey Mildew
8. Fusarium Wilt
9. Crown Gall
10. Nematodes

1. Scales

Scales are tiny red insects which affect rose plants by sucking the cell content from the leaves leading to yellowing of rose foliage, wilting of the plant and dying of rose seedlings.

Scales should be controlled by removing and destroying infested parts by scales and by spraying rose plants with white mineral oils.

2. Spider Mites

Spider Mites are red oval insects which feed on rose plant leaves leading to silvery appearance and drying of the leaves.

Spider Mites may be controlled by ensuring that rose plants are weeded early.

3. White Flies

White Flies are tiny long insects with white bodies that have waxy appearance. White flies feed on rose plants leading to wilting of the plants, yellowing of the leaves and eventual dying of the plant.

White flies may be controlled chemically by spraying them with insecticides like Deltamethrin.

4. Mealybugs

Mealybugs are tiny insects with flat bodies which affect rose plants by sucking the cell sap content like scales leading to yellowing of foliage and sooty molds on rose plants.

Mealybugs can be controlled by removing and burning affected parts and by spraying affected parts with insecticides.

5. Thrips

Thrips are tiny slender insects which affect the plant tissues of rose plants leading to brownish appearance and eventual dying of the plant tissues.

Thrips may be treated chemically by spraying them with insecticides as recommended by a veterinarian.

6. Powdery Mildew

Powdery Mildew is a fungal disease which survives in buds of rose plants and can easily destroy the plants if undetected early.

Powdery Mildew produces powdery growths on flowers, foliage and flower petals. Powdery Mildew may lead to grayish lesions on foliage and flower distortion.

Powdery Mildew may be controlled by maintain quality standards in the planting area like spacing and weeding. Powdery Mildew may be treated by spraying Neem oil to the infested parts.

7. Downey Mildew

Downey Mildew is a fungal disease which is popular in soils that are not properly drained.

Downey Mildew may lead to lesions formation on rose plant foliage and shrinking of growing tips.

Downey Mildew may be controlled by ensuring that rose plants are free from weeds .

8. Fusarium Wilt

Fusarium Wilt is a soil borne disease which affects rose plants resulting in yellowing of rose foliage, brown discoloration on plant tissues and wilting of the vines of the plant.

Fusarium Wilt disease can be controlled by keeping rose plants free from weeds and by planting rose plants which are resistant to diseases.

9. Crown Gall

Crown Gall is a soil borne disease which can affect rose plants leading to improper growth rates of rose plants and formation of galls on the roots. Crown Gall may lead to slow growth rates of rose plants and introducing control measures at the farm may help in keeping the plants safe.

Crown Gall may be controlled by ensuring that planting and pruning materials are sterilized before and after use.

10. Nematodes

Nematodes are soil borne diseases which can be easily spread by planting materials which have not been disinfected or through infected seedlings.

Rose plants affected by nematodes may have yellowish leaves, roots distortion, swollen roots and wilted plants.

Nematodes may be controlled by ensuring that planting materials are disinfected with chlorine solution before using them and after using them.

ABOUT THE AUTHOR

Davies Cheruiyot is an agribusiness specialist with a degree in agribusiness. He turned to farming in 2015 to expand his knowledge on agriculture. He is the author of Growing Hydrangeas, Growing Peonies, Growing Dragon Fruits, Growing Strawberries and several other books

Printed in Dunstable, United Kingdom